FISHER
BIBLE STUDYGUIDE

Spiritual
Disciplines

The Tasks of a Joyful Life

L A R R Y   S I B L E Y

SHAW BOOKS

an imprint of WATERBROOK PRESS

Spiritual Disciplines
A SHAW BOOK
PUBLISHED BY WATERBROOK PRESS
2375 Telstar Drive, Suite 160
Colorado Springs, Colorado 80920
A division of Random House, Inc.

ISBN 0-87788-036-0

Printed in the United States of America
2004

10 9 8 7 6 5 4 3 2

Contents

How to Use This Studyguide

isherman studyguides are based on the inductive approach to Bible study. Inductive study is discovery study; we discover what the Bible says as we ask questions about its content and search for answers. This is quite different from the process in which a teacher *tells* a group *about* the Bible—what it means and what to do about it. In inductive study, God speaks directly to each of us through his Word.

A group functions best when a leader keeps the discussion on target, but the leader is neither the teacher nor the "answer person." A leader's responsibility is to *ask*—not *tell*. The answers come from the text itself as group members examine, discuss, and think together about the passage.

There are four kinds of questions in each study. The first is an *approach question*. Asked and answered before the Bible passage is read, this question breaks the ice and helps you start thinking about the topic of the Bible study. It begins to reveal where thoughts and feelings need to be transformed by Scripture.

Some of the earlier questions in each study are *observation questions*—who, what, where, when, and how—designed to help you learn some basic facts about the passage of Scripture.

Once you know what the Bible says, you need to ask, *What does it mean?* These *interpretation questions* help you discover the writer's basic message.

Next come *application questions,* which ask, *What does it mean to me?* They challenge you to live out the Scripture's life-transforming message.

Fisherman studyguides provide spaces between questions for jotting down responses as well as any related questions you would like to raise in the group. Each group member should have a copy of the studyguide and may take a turn in leading the group.

A group should use any accurate, modern translation of the Bible such as the *New International Version,* the *New American Standard Bible,* the *New Living Translation,* the *New Revised Standard Version,* the *New Jerusalem Bible,* or the *Good News Bible.* (Other translations or paraphrases of the Bible may be referred to when additional help is needed.) Bible commentaries should not be brought to a Bible study because they tend to dampen discussion and keep people from thinking for themselves.

SUGGESTIONS FOR GROUP LEADERS

1. Thoroughly read and study the Bible passage before the meeting. Get a firm grasp on its themes and begin applying its teachings for yourself. Pray that the Holy Spirit will "guide you into all truth" (John 16:13) so that your leadership will guide others.

2. If any of the studyguide's questions seem ambiguous or unnatural to you, rephrase them, feeling free to add others that seem necessary to bring out the meaning of a verse.

3. Begin (and end) the study promptly. Start by asking someone to pray that every participant will both understand the passage and be open to its transforming power. Remember, the Holy Spirit is the teacher, not you!

4. Ask for volunteers to read the passages aloud.

5. As you ask the studyguide's questions in sequence, encourage everyone to participate in the discussion. If some are silent, try gently suggesting, "Let's have an answer from someone who hasn't spoken up yet."

6. If a question comes up that you can't answer, don't be afraid to admit that you're baffled. Assign the topic as a research project for someone to report on next week, or say, "I'll do some studying and let you know what I find out."

7. Keep the discussion moving, but be sure it stays focused. Though a certain number of tangents are inevitable, you'll want to quickly bring the discussion back to the topic at hand. Also, learn to pace the discussion so that you finish the lesson in the time allotted.

8. Don't be afraid of silences; some questions take time to answer, and some people need time to gather courage to speak. If silence persists, rephrase your question, but resist the temptation to answer it yourself.

9. If someone comes up with an answer that is clearly illogical or unbiblical, ask for further clarification: "What verse suggests that to you?"

10. Discourage overuse of cross references. Learn all you can from the passage at hand, while selectively incorporating a few important references suggested in the studyguide.

11. Some questions are marked with a ✐. This indicates that further information is available in the Leader's Notes at the back of the guide.

12. For more information on getting a new Bible study group started and keeping it functioning effectively, read *You Can Start a Bible Study Group* by Gladys M. Hunt and *Pilgrims in Progress: Growing Through Groups* by Jim and Carol Plueddemann. (Both books are available from Shaw Books.)

Suggestions for Group Members

1. Learn and apply the following ground rules for effective Bible study. (If new members join the group later, review these guidelines with the whole group.)

2. Remember that your goal is to learn all you can *from the Bible passage being studied.* Let it speak for itself without using Bible commentaries or other Bible passages. There is more than enough in each assigned passage to keep your group productively occupied for one session. Sticking to the passage saves the group from insecurity ("I don't have the right reference books—or the time to read anything else.") and confusion ("Where did *that* come from? I thought we were studying _____.").

3. Avoid the temptation to bring up those fascinating tangents that don't really grow out of the passage you are discussing. If the topic is of common interest, you can bring it up later in informal conversation after the study. Meanwhile, help one another stick to the subject.

4. Encourage one another to participate. People remember best what they discover and verbalize for

themselves. Some people are naturally shy, while others may be afraid of making a mistake. If your discussion is free and friendly and you show real interest in what other group members think and feel, the quieter ones will be more likely to speak up. Remember, the more people involved in a discussion, the richer it will be.

5. Guard yourself from answering too many questions or talking too much. Give others a chance to share their ideas. If you are one who participates easily, discipline yourself by counting to ten before you open your mouth.

6. Make personal, honest applications and commit yourself to letting God's Word change you.

Introduction

S piritual discipline" has a grim, rigorous ring to it. Is this just one more element of the "Church of Perpetual Obligation," as author Garrison Keillor calls it? Or is spiritual discipline an essential and joyful means of grace for believers? Richard Foster thinks it is the latter. In his book *Celebration of Discipline*, he states: "The inner righteousness we seek is not something that is poured on our heads. God has ordained the disciplines of the spiritual life as the means by which we place ourselves where he can bless us."

The spiritual disciplines have a long history in the Christian church. Paul wrote about disciplining his body to keep his spiritual life healthy (see 1 Corinthians 9:25-27). He also urged Timothy to be diligent in disciplining himself and in reading and preaching the Word to others (see 1 Timothy 4:7-8,11-13). In the third and fourth centuries, the Desert Fathers and Mothers sought to clear away the distractions to spiritual growth and purity through consistent prayer, meditation, fasting, and solitude. Monasticism promoted this growth through a communal round of daily prayers, Scripture reading, the Lord's Supper, and meditation balanced by study and work. At the time of the Reformation, Lutherans and Calvinists developed the idea of the "means of grace"—the word, prayer, and the sacraments—as God's normal way of helping us grow into conformity to Christ.

There never has been an official list of spiritual disciplines. The trio of "word, prayer, and sacraments" comes closest because the Westminster Assembly adopted it in the seventeenth century as the standard for British and Scottish Christians. As we focus on these disciplines, we come to know God better, become holier, and become better equipped to serve him. They do not produce spiritual health all by themselves; rather, they are the means that God often chooses to help us grow. As in all areas of our spiritual growth, these disciplines produce fruit only as we trust God's Holy Spirit to work through them in our lives.

We have selected eight of the most basic and common disciplines for spiritual growth for your study in this guide. They are certainly enough to get you started, perhaps even more than you think you can manage right now. As you discuss these disciplines in your small group or work through them alone, you will discover that they really do quicken your spiritual life. They are indeed the disciplines of a joyful life!

Waiting: Time for God

ISAIAH 30:15-18

Technical civilization is man's conquest
of space. It is a triumph frequently achieved
by sacrificing an essential ingredient of
existence, namely, time. In technical
civilization, we expend time to gain space....
But time is the art of existence.

—ABRAHAM JOSHUA HESCHEL, *The Sabbath*

Time is a valuable commodity, at the least. How we use our time shows what we value. As we begin this study on the spiritual disciplines, it is good to take a look at how we spend our days. It's so easy to feel productive as we rush around *doing*—working on projects, shuttling the kids to activities, serving on committees, going to church—that we can lose our sense of *being*. That's when we need to slow down, remember our priorities, and make time for God.

1. What are the three most urgent *demands* on your time? What are your three most urgent time *needs?*

READ ISAIAH 30:15-18.

⊘ 2. What do you learn about the speaker in verse 15?

3. According to this passage, what are the ways to salvation and strength?

4. How are the attitudes and actions listed in verse 15 similar yet different?

⊘ *Indicates further information in Leader's Notes*

✐ 5. How did the people of Isaiah's day respond to God's message (verse 16)?

How did their preferred course of action contrast with God's way to salvation?

6. How would you paraphrase "flee on horses" to reflect modern ways of escaping difficulties?

In what ways do you try to run from trouble instead of resting in God?

7. What did the prophet say would be the result of the people's choices (verses 16-17)?

8. In verse 18, what is God's desire and action? What kind of God is he?

9. How does the end of verse 18 echo verse 15?

10. In what ways are waiting and resting related?

✐ 11. The word *wait* appears several times in Isaiah. What do the following verses add to your understanding of what it means to wait on God?

Isaiah 8:17

Isaiah 64:4

12. Where does time for God rank in your priorities? Explain.

✐ *Journal Exercise*

As you begin this studyguide, you may want to set some simple goals for spending regular time with God. Ask yourself, When will I work through this guide each week? Where? What new skills and attitudes would I like to develop? What do I need to do to make more time and space for God in my life? Write down your goals to help you confirm your commitment. Then ask God to help you grow in your desire to wait on him and rest in him:

> O God of peace, who has taught us that in returning and rest we shall be saved, in quietness and in confidence shall be our strength: By the might of your Spirit lift us, we pray, to your presence, where we may be still and know that you are God; through Jesus Christ our Lord. Amen.
> *(The Book of Common Prayer)*

Meditation: Soaking Up God's Word

PSALM 77

*The Word of Scripture should never stop
sounding in your ears and working in you all
day long, just like the words of someone you
love. And just as you do not analyze the words
of someone you love, but accept them as they
are said to you, accept the Word of Scripture
and ponder it in your heart, as Mary did.
That is all. That is meditation...ponder this
Word long in your heart until it has gone right
into you and taken possession of you.*

—DIETRICH BONHOEFFER, *The Way to Freedom*

otice how focused Bonhoeffer's description of meditation is. It can be as simple as taking a key phrase or verse
from your Bible reading in the morning and letting it work in
you all day. Christian meditation is content-oriented—filling
the mind and heart with Scripture—in contrast to Eastern

meditation, which seeks to empty the mind. As we ponder what God has said and shape our lives around that, we are transformed.

✐ 1. Write a short description of what you think meditation looks like. What do you think a person might do while meditating?

READ PSALM 77:1-9.

2. List the psalmist's actions in verses 1-6. What do the verbs tell you?

3. In what ways are verses 1 and 3 similar?

What does verse 3 add to the picture?

4. What six questions did the writer ask in verses 7-9? What do these questions reveal about the psalmist's state of mind and heart?

5. How does this rush of questions fit with the situation you discovered in verses 2 and 4?

 6. Summarize the psalmist's situation here. How did he handle it?

7. Have you ever had a similar experience? If you wish, describe it briefly.

Read Psalm 77:10-20.

✎ 8. To what did the psalmist finally appeal in verses
      10-12?

      What is the significance of the pronoun change
      from "I" to "you"?

9.   List the verbs in verses 10-12. What activity do they
      describe?

10.   In what way do the memories listed in verses 12-15
      contrast with the questions of verses 7-9?

      To what do you attribute the psalmist's shift in
      viewpoint?

✐ 11. What redemptive deeds and works of the Lord did the psalmist remember (verses 16-20)?

12. What do you learn about the discipline of meditation from this psalm?

Journal Exercise

Have you recently been in a dire personal situation like that faced by the psalmist? Or have you ever been overwhelmed by the suffering of others in some part of the world? How can meditating on who God is and on his Word help you during such times? Write your thoughts about this in your journal.

Singing historical psalms (such as Psalm 105), hymns, and praise songs; hearing the Scripture readings in worship services; and reciting creeds and prayers are ways of meditating aloud with other believers. When you attend worship this week, note how any one of these elements reminds you of God's works in an encouraging way, then write a few sentences about this in your journal.

Prayer: Coming into God's Presence

ISAIAH 37:9-20,36-37; ACTS 4:23-31

*Does anyone have the foggiest idea what sort of
power we so blithely invoke? Or, as I suspect,
does no one believe a word of it? The churches
are children playing on the floor with their
chemistry sets, mixing up a batch of TNT
to kill a Sunday morning. It is madness to
wear ladies' straw hats and velvet hats to
church; we should all be wearing crash helmets.*

—ANNIE DILLARD, *Teaching a Stone to Talk*

S ome prayers begin with "Almighty God" or "Sovereign
Lord;" others start with "Lord" or "Lord God." But we
often breeze right by the opening as if it were just the paint on
the door of a prayer room. Yet, as Annie Dillard observed,
coming into God's presence is more like entering a hard-hat
zone. God welcomes us, to be sure, but he is not a tame God;
he is more like a lion, a strong wind, an awesome ruler.

In this study we will look carefully at how a king (Hezekiah) and the early church approached God, how they showed their awareness of his awesome presence and yet approached him confidently. Prayer, even as a regular discipline, should never become a mere routine, a safe practice-run. It's real-time, working with the power on. So how can we find the right balance between awe and confidence when we pray? As we study these passages from Isaiah and Acts, we will be looking for clues.

1. How do you picture God? As a cuddly grandfather? a raging storm? an indifferent stranger? Explain.

READ ISAIAH 37:9-20, 36-37.

2. Briefly describe the situation in this passage. Who and what threatened King Hezekiah?

3. What was Hezekiah's response to the threat (verses 14-15)?

✎ 4. As Hezekiah prayed, what name did he use to address God?

What other descriptions of God did he use?

✎ 5. How much of Hezekiah's prayer was devoted to the actual request, and how much to describing and praising God? What does this reveal about his understanding of prayer?

READ ACTS 4:23-31.

✎ 6. What threat did the early church in Jerusalem face?

How was this threat similar to the threat that Hezekiah and ancient Jerusalem faced?

↗ 7. How did these early Christians begin their prayer (verse 24)?

8. In verses 25 and 26, the believers quoted Psalm 2:1-2 as part of their prayer. How are these words appropriate to their situation?

9. What is most threatening to you at present?

How can you apply the truths of Psalm 2, as the early Christians did, to this situation?

10. Compare verse 29 with verse 31. What happened as a result of the believers' prayer?

11. Do you pray expecting that God will answer you
    as clearly as he did Hezekiah and the early church?
    Why or why not?

⌁ 12. The early church used the psalms as prayers and
    songs. We sometimes find written prayers boring
    or restricting. How could we use God's Word, the
    psalms in particular, to guide our praying?

Journal Exercise

Before you begin to pray each day, meditate for a few minutes
on Psalm 43:3. This will increase your awareness of God's presence as you pray. In your journal, record your thoughts about
coming to the place where God dwells.

Use Psalm 8 as a prayer this week, paraphrasing it to express praise for God as you see his work in the world. Include
the concerns and persons for whom you would normally pray.
Write these prayers in your journal.

Fasting: Hunger That Satisfies

MATTHEW 6:1-8,16-18

*When the flesh is satisfied it is hard to pray
with cheerfulness or to devote oneself to a life of
service, which calls for much self-renunciation.*
—DIETRICH BONHOEFFER, *The Cost of Discipleship*

In our advertising-saturated culture, we can no longer easily distinguish between what we need and what we want. Television commercials and magazine ads promote every product or service as an answer to a need. Actually, our needs are few: God; the companionship of family, friends, and members of the body of Christ; adequate food, clothing, and shelter; meaningful work; and Sabbath rest. Can you add much to that list?

Because our physical needs and wants can obscure our relationship with God, fasting has been used in the church to clear away the clutter of our needs and desires and provide special times of focused attention on God. It's not that food is evil;

it's necessary, and God has given us all things to enjoy. Yet, for some people at some times, it can be beneficial to abstain from eating for a while in order to pray. Let's see what Jesus had to say about this topic.

✐ 1. List all the things you did in the past twenty-four hours to satisfy your physical needs.

READ MATTHEW 6:1-8,16-18.

2. In these verses, Jesus spoke of three "acts of right-eousness." What are they?

3. Summarize Jesus' main point in verses 1-8.

✳ 4. Who knows what we need (verse 8)?

How can this fact help you assess what you need and separate those needs from your wants?

5. What clues do you find in verses 16-18 that Jesus expected his disciples to fast (see also Matthew 9:15)?

✳ 6. Before whom should we fast? From whom should we keep it hidden?

Why do you think we should keep these two separate?

 7. What do giving, praying, and fasting have in common in this passage?

How are they different?

 8. How does our heavenly Father respond to secret acts of righteousness?

 9. How many times is God called "Father" in these verses?

What does this tell you about the discipline of fasting?

✐ 10. If fasting is to be secret—for God our Father—the main benefits must be his, not ours. What do you think pleases God about fasting?

✐ 11. What practical obstacles would you face in practicing the discipline of fasting?

Note: To supplement your own list, talk to someone who maintains this discipline or read a good book such as *Celebration of Discipline* by Richard Foster or one of the other resources listed in the Suggested Reading section at the end of this study. WARNING: Do not just plunge in on your own. This discipline needs expert guidance from a doctor or a spiritual leader. Seek it and follow it.

Journal Exercise
Read, meditate on, and pray through Psalms 42 and 43. Look for images of fasting (i.e., hunger, thirst) and feasting or celebrating. Notice how these images focus on desiring God and finding satisfaction in him. Write your thoughts and prayers in your journal.

You may find the following prayer helpful as you enter your quiet time. Journal about your own "coldness of heart and wanderings of mind," identifying the problem so that you can ask God to help you desire him above all.

O Almighty God, who pours out on all who desire it the spirit of grace and of supplication: Deliver us, when we draw near to you, from coldness of heart and wanderings of mind, that with steadfast thoughts and kindled affections we may worship you in spirit and in truth; through Jesus Christ our Lord. Amen. *(The Book of Common Prayer)*

Solitude: The Nourishing Quiet

LUKE 4:31-44; 5:15-16; 9:10-17

Instead of running away from our loneliness
and trying to forget or deny it, we have to
protect it and turn it into a fruitful solitude.
To live a spiritual life we must first find the
courage to enter into the desert of our loneliness
and to change it by gentle and persistent
efforts into a garden of solitude.
—HENRI NOUWEN, *Reaching Out*

There is an epidemic of loneliness in our culture. Fear of being alone leads to frenzied activity, noise ("there's no music here"), and grasping, suffocating relationships. Solitude seems more like a desert than the garden Jesus enjoyed in the passages we will explore in this study. Withdrawal from the distracting world is helpful at times. Isolation develops solitude of heart, an inner quality of sensitivity to God, to others, and to oneself. Solitude (instead of loneliness) comes from having been loved by God and by parents, siblings, friends, or one's spouse.

1. The last time you were faced with solitude, were you able to welcome it as a friend, or did you shy away from it as a threat? Explain.

READ LUKE 4:31-44.

✐ 2. How would you describe Jesus' "workload" that day—light, medium, or heavy?

3. List Jesus' activities described in verses 31-37. On a scale from 1 (least) to 10 (most), estimate the physical energy drain for each activity.

4. What happened at the end of the day (verses 38-41)?

How might these things have further drained Jesus' energy?

5. What did Jesus' actions early the next morning (verse 42) suggest about his priorities?

6. What further clues about his priorities do you find in verse 43?

In what way do you think Jesus' decision was influenced by the way he started the day?

READ LUKE 5:15-16.

⚘ 7. What similarities to the previous passage do you find?

What new elements or facts did Luke add here?

8. Summarize what you have learned about Jesus' use of solitude thus far.

READ LUKE 9:10-17.

9. Following a busy time of ministry, what did Jesus do with his disciples (verse 10)? Why?

10. Identify the different ways in which the people were "fed" by Jesus (verses 11,12-17).

✄ 11. How are these two ways of being fed related to each other?

In what ways have you been nourished physically and spiritually this past week?

12. Think about the last busy, terrible-horrible-no-good-very-bad day you had. How did you feel the next morning?

Why would a time of solitude with God help as you begin that kind of no-good-very-bad day?

Journal Exercise

A crucial part of effective solitude is the right place. If you don't have such a place, make finding one a priority. Exchange ideas with the members of your group. Be creative.

As you begin your quiet times this week, read Psalm 62. Write in your journal what you learn about silence or solitude from this psalm. Then meditate on the following verse for five minutes, letting silence settle around you: "The LORD is in his holy temple; let all the earth be silent before him" (Habakkuk 2:20).

Spiritual Direction: Receiving Encouragement

2 TIMOTHY 3:1-17

*[In the early church] faith involved far
more than an intellectual assent to the
historical validity of Christ's work; as Jesus had
said, it was a commitment to follow him—to
walk in his steps. Appropriately, then,
Christianity came to be described as "the Way."*

—ROBERT COLEMAN, *The Master Plan of Discipleship*

By the time Timothy read this letter from Paul, his mentor, he had been walking all over Turkey and Greece with Paul, literally following in Paul's footsteps. When you think about it, learning firsthand about the Christian life from a godly mentor is much more satifying than reading about it in a book or two. Books help, but a real-life example shows you what discipleship looks like, even what Christ looks like, in another human being. You get feedback, evaluation, and encouragement, and you have someone to come alongside to listen, guide, and demonstrate.

If the Christian life is "the Way," then we toddlers need a mature walker or two to encourage us along the journey. Although not practiced widely today, this spiritual discipline should be a normal part of growing in the Christian life, a discipline that's also a helping friendship.

1. How can you learn to walk in Christ's steps when you can't see him?

READ 2 TIMOTHY 3:1-9.

2. What kind of people did Paul warn Timothy about in verses 2-5?

Which of these characteristics do you see in today's news headlines, in yourself, or in someone you know?

3. What problems do you think Timothy would have faced as a Christian when he encountered these attitudes in his community?

4. Verses 6-8 give us examples of some behaviors that were intruding into the early church. What challenges would Timothy have faced as a church leader seeking to disciple new converts from this kind of society? (See 2 Timothy 2:24-25 for Paul's advice to Timothy.)

READ 2 TIMOTHY 3:10-17.

5. Describe the kind of role model Paul was to Timothy (verses 10-11).

✐ 6.   What was Timothy's attitude toward Paul's example (verse 14)?

7.   List the personal experiences Paul described in verses 10-13. How would this information help Timothy with the challenges he faced?

✐ 8.   What earlier role models did Timothy have (verse 15)?

9.   To what source of wisdom did these examples point (verses 15-17)?

10.   What qualities of Scripture did Paul list in verse 16?

Why do we need Scripture in our lives (verse 17)?

11. How have these qualities of God's Word been medi-
ated to you through mentors, family, or friends?

✐ 12. If you don't currently have a spiritual model or
mentor, who might perform this service for Christ
in your life? List three possibilities and begin to pray
about approaching one of these people about mentoring you in the Scriptures and in your spiritual
growth.

Journal Exercise
As you think about receiving spiritual direction, read through
Psalm 15. This psalm explores godly character as displayed in
thoughts, prayers, and actions. Write down the traits and attitudes that you would like to see in a spiritual mentor as well as
in your own life. Paraphrase the psalm into a prayer, asking
God to make you more godly in these ways.

The Sabbath: Time of Renewal

ISAIAH 56:1-8; 58:13-14

*How do you slice your time? One tool is
the word no. No is a knife word....
The ancient Chinese philosopher Mencius
once said, "Before a man can do things,
there must be things he will not do."*

—MIRIAM ADENEY, *A Time for Risking*

We live in a society that values productivity. We often use
the phrase *24/7* to describe a supposedly successful lifestyle that is full of pressure, accomplishment, and, perhaps,
fun. There is usually little downtime. Every moment—even
riding a bike on Sunday afternoon—has to produce something. We do this to ourselves, and we expect everyone else
to follow along. Soon people begin to burn out, and they are
pushed aside as unproductive.

The hidden assumption in all this activity is that our
time is *ours* to do with as we wish. The Bible challenges that

assumption. When we honor God's ownership of our time, we will know better when to say yes and when to say no. We also discover that he has given us a great gift: the Sabbath.

1. How do you "slice" your time and decide how to spend it?

Read Isaiah 56:1-8.

2. Along with keeping the Sabbath, what other practices for eunuchs and foreigners are mentioned here (verses 2,4,6)?

✐ 3. Compare verse 1 with verse 2. How would maintaining justice and keeping the Sabbath reinforce each other?

✐ 4. What were the eunuchs and foreigners afraid of (verse 3)?

How did God's promises speak to their fears (verses 5,7)?

✐ 5. In a 24/7 workworld such as we sometimes have today, how do these promises free us to know God and enjoy him?

6. What did God expect or ask from each group (verses 4,6)?

✐ 7. What role would these outcast groups have in maintaining justice?

What contemporary counterparts of these groups can you suggest?

READ ISAIAH 58:13-14.

8. What additional insights do you find here about what it means to keep the Sabbath?

✐ 9. What attitudes, negative and positive, are mentioned here that would hinder or help you in keeping the Sabbath?

10. What blessings are promised to those who "delight" in the Sabbath?

⌀ 11. What can you do with a group of Christians to
       make the Sabbath (usually Sunday) a delight?

12. As you think about what you have learned from
     these passages in Isaiah, how do they encourage you
     to make keeping the Sabbath your top priority?

Journal Exercise

This week try putting the Lord's Day at the center of your
week, taking three days to anticipate its joys, and then three
days to savor what you enjoyed.

Read the psalms that are suggested on the following page
for each day of the week, starting with Thursday. Write in your
journal how they lead up to and follow from the worship celebration on Sunday. (Did Thursday's psalm get you thinking
ahead to Sunday's worship? Friday's psalm relates Jesus' medi-
tations as he hung on the cross; how did Saturday's psalm
anticipate the Resurrection? How did the psalm for Sunday
prepare you to celebrate? How was Monday's psalm fitting for

the start of the workweek?) This journal exercise is a bit more complicated than previous ones, but it's well worth the effort to help you enjoy the Sabbath (Sunday).

Thursday—Psalm 18
Friday—Psalm 22
Saturday—Psalm 20
The Lord's Day—Psalms 148–150
Monday—Psalm 25
Tuesday—Psalm 26
Wednesday—Psalm 38

Worship: Going to Jerusalem

HEBREWS 12:18-24,28-29

Pictures of heavenly worship, led by angels in chorus, are not immediately relevant to our times. Worship defined in a way that suggests a correlation between two worlds, ours and God's, has a hard time making sense to those in our society for whom the "real" world is exactly the one they can see, touch, and use.
—RALPH P. MARTIN, *The Worship of God*

W orship, like the other spiritual disciplines we've been exploring, involves a pattern of spiritual exercise, often repetitive, but cumulative in its effect. As we enter into worship each week, amazing things happen. All the time we've spent with God in solitude and prayer, in Bible reading and meditation, in self-discipline and fasting, as well as the spiritual direction and the Sabbath renewal we've received, come together in sharper focus as we join the assembly of Christians in worship.

The people who received the letter to the Hebrews needed to be refreshed with the realization that they were part of something very big and otherworldly. We, too, need to be aware of the glorious unseen realities as we worship.

1. How does worship help you remember the things you cannot see?

READ HEBREWS 12:18-24.

⌀ 2. List the "touchable" aspects of the first scene (verses 18-21).

Would you want to touch or experience any of them? Why or why not?

3. Describe the overall atmosphere found at Mount Sinai.

4. What are the unseen, "untouchable" aspects of the second mountain (verses 22-24)?

♪ 5. What word(s) summarize the contrasting atmospheres at Mount Sinai and Mount Zion?

6. What other differences do you notice between the two places?

7. List the inhabitants of the city of God (verses 22-24).

Who are the central figures there?

✒ 8. What event mentioned in verse 24 best explains the change that takes place when we move from one "mountain" of God's presence to the other?

READ HEBREWS 12:28-29.

9. With what attitudes are we to worship God? Why?

✒ 10. What do you think it would be like to participate in this scene in the heavenly Jerusalem? What aspects of the heavenly Jerusalem have you recently discovered in your personal worship?

11. How can these unseen realities affect your times of worship?

Journal Exercise

This week read one of these praise psalms (Psalms 146–150) each day, and in your journal describe the scene in each. What happened? Who participated? How did worship occur? What musical instruments were used? What sights, sounds, and smells, do you notice? How are these elements reflected in the various parts of worship at your church? Choose one psalm and meditate on it in preparation for worship this coming Sunday.

Leader's Notes

STUDY 1: WAITING

Purpose:
- To see the importance of time spent with God, actively trusting and resting in him.
- To schedule a regular time for completing the study questions and journal exercises in this guide.

Question 2. Isaiah was a prophet living in Jerusalem during the eighth century before Christ. Since he was called to this office at the death of Uzziah (see Isaiah 6:1), we can date his work from 740 B.C. to about 700 B.C., or perhaps later. He emphasized the holiness of God, God's demands for holiness in his people, and the promise of a coming Servant who would purify the people.

Question 5. The emphasis on *resting, trusting,* and *waiting* contrasts with *fleeing* in the text. It also contradicts our activist natures—"Don't just stand there; *do* something!"—by telling us to wait and rest—"Don't just do something; *stand* there!" The answer is not mere inactivity, but resting in God, who will act through us and for us.

Question 11. Isaiah used the word *wait* in several other places, but these two verses have been selected because the same Hebrew word *(châkâh)* appears. The tone of the word here is "quiet expectation." Isaiah used other Hebrew words for "wait" that convey a much more intense kind of waiting, like that of a tightly twisted rope *(qâwâh;* Isaiah 25:9, "trusted"; 40:31, "hope"), or of more eager anticipation (*yâchal;* Isaiah 42:4, "hope"). As you can see, the *New International Version* translates these words in various ways. Suggest to group members that they insert the word *wait* in all these verses, to see how that opens up the meaning. We can wait quietly, or we can trust and hope intensely or with anticipation.

Journal Exercise. Journaling—writing out your thoughts and prayers on paper—is not to be just another task to do, but rather a suggested way to cultivate a parallel discipline, one that will make all the other spiritual disciplines more effective. Encourage those group members who want to journal to set modest goals as they begin: maybe writing two or three sentences at first, just enough to crystallize their thoughts. As time goes on, they may want to write more.

Note: If group members wish, discuss some specific steps they can take in this process of setting goals for the spiritual disciplines. Elicit some examples of new skills or attitudes. Talk about places to study, ways to explore the disciplines, and how to pace themselves. This discussion will make things more concrete and help group members as they work privately on further application.

Study 2: Meditation

Purpose:
- To remove misconceptions about meditation by focusing on a biblical model.
- To deal with painful experiences by meditating on God's words and works.

Question 1. It's important to emphasize to the group that biblical meditation is an attempt to fill the mind with truth, in contrast to the meditation of Eastern religions, which is an attempt to empty the mind. In Luke 11:24-26, Jesus warned about the danger facing the person who is emptied of evil but not filled with good.

Question 6. The psalmist described sleepless nights of prayer and meditation, waiting for God to help with his problem and questioning whether God cared or had forgotten. Help the group appreciate the honesty of these feelings.

Question 8. The process that the psalmist goes through here is similar to mulling over an experience or talking to oneself about a problem in order to clarify one's thinking. The psalmist shows us a healthy way to "talk to oneself." Note how the dominant pronoun shifted from "I" to "you" as the psalmist focused on God.

Question 11. The writer remembered the miraculous Exodus events (see Exodus 14:19-31). Notice how the historical and poetic versions mesh. God's actions redeemed his people from the idols of the Egyptians (see Exodus 12:12) and also freed them from political bondage.

Study 3: Prayer

Purpose:
   • To believe more fully that prayer brings us into God's presence in a special way, and to become more aware of his majesty and glory.

• To develop a habit of using set forms of prayer
(such as a psalm or a prayer text) as a biblical way
to pray.

Question 4. As you prepare to lead, read the passages about
Hezekiah in 2 Kings 18–19 and Isaiah 36–37 to get a more
complete picture of the background for Hezekiah's prayer.

Question 5. The definition of *praise* in the *Webster's New Colle-
giate Dictionary* is "to express a favorable judgment of…by the
attribution of perfections." Hezekiah praised God by describing his attributes, his character, and his actions.

Question 6. Acts 4:1-22 provides background for the prayer in
verse 24 and the verses that follow. Make as complete a list as
you can of the parallels to Hezekiah's experience, then select
the most significant one. This will help you guide the group
quickly through the first part of this question.

Question 7. "Sovereign Lord,…you made the heaven" (Acts
4:24) is based on Exodus 20:11 and Psalm 146:6. The phrase
"Stretch out your hand" (4:30) is based on Exodus 3:20. The
prayer is filled with biblical (Old Testament) language.

Question 12. Make sure the group realizes how easily the early
church incorporated the psalms into their prayers. They mem-
orized and recited the Word of God. When they were under
pressure, their earlier habits helped them pray. Sometimes a
prepared prayer that uses biblical language can be better than
one said "off the cuff."

Study 4: Fasting

Purpose:
- To understand that fasting is a gift we offer to God.
- To carefully prepare ourselves before beginning the discipline of fasting.

Question 1. Ask several group members to share one "need." Then ask, "Were these really needs, or were they wants?" Discuss how our wants can seem like needs in our advertising-saturated culture.

Question 4. Looking back at the Beatitudes (Matthew 5:3-12), notice all the blessings promised to those who are deprived of the things we take for granted. This passage is part of the context for understanding God's fatherly care of his people as they sort out their needs and wants, and as they fast.

Question 6. The point Jesus was making is that fasting is for God to see; it is primarily for his pleasure. There are benefits for us—a clearer spiritual focus, time to pray, better health—but these are secondary.

Question 7. The immediate context of Matthew 6:16-18 (fasting) is Jesus' teaching about prayer and giving to others. All are primarily for God, but they also affect human beings in different ways.

Question 9. Take time to probe various facets of God's character as Father—the Source of life and our life support, his loving concern for our growth, our strong shelter—as these relate to the discipline, challenges, and risks of fasting.

Question 10. Help your group look at fasting from God's point of view. For instance, how do you react when someone misses a meal in order to see you?

Question 11. As you discuss the possibility of fasting, stress the health and medical risks involved. Some people, perhaps most, should check with their doctors first. Everyone should read about the physiological effects in order to be fully prepared. Chapter 4 of Richard Foster's book *Celebration of Discipline* gives a good overview.

STUDY 5: SOLITUDE

Purpose:
- To learn from Jesus' example the importance of silence and solitude as a spiritual discipline.
- To strengthen the discipline of a daily "quiet time."

Question 2. "Jesus had recently moved to Capernaum from Nazareth (Matthew 4:13). Capernaum was a thriving city.… Because it was the headquarters for many Roman troops, word about Jesus could spread all over the Roman empire" (*Life Application Bible,* Wheaton, Ill.: Tyndale, 1991, p. 1801).

Question 7. In Luke 4:42, Luke reported that Jesus went "to a solitary place." In Luke 5:16, he added the word "often" and the fact that Jesus "prayed." (Although some translations do not include the word "often," the *New International Version* uses it to express the force of an iterative imperfect in the Greek for "withdrew"; in other words, it was his regular pattern).

Question 11. God meets both our spiritual and physical needs. It's interesting to note that this passage features the main elements found in a worship service: the Word (Christ's teaching) and the Lord's Supper (bread). Explore these possibilities. John 6 is a helpful passage with similar content.

STUDY 6: SPIRITUAL DIRECTION

Purpose:
- To learn that one way to develop Christian character is through following the life examples of role models and mentors.
- To encourage group members to seek out a mentor or spiritual director if they do not already have one.

Question 5. The apostle Paul first met Timothy in Lystra (near modern-day Katyn Serai, Turkey) and invited him to join Paul's missionary team (see Acts 16:1-3). During the next few years, Paul mentored Timothy as they worked together to bring the gospel to the peoples of Asia (now Turkey) and Greece. Paul was in Rome, near the end of his life (A.D. 65–67), when he wrote this second letter to Timothy.

Question 6. Paul reminded Timothy how he had closely followed (knew all about) Paul's practices and purposes. The Greek word Paul used *(parēkolouthēsas)* implies paying close attention in order to learn. Timothy actively watched and received Paul's example.

Question 8. See 2 Timothy 1:5 for Timothy's background. Family members also help form our characters and lead us to the Word.

Question 12. As you discuss the importance of having role models and mentors in our lives, it may be helpful to mention some criteria for choosing a spiritual director. This person should have a greater level of spiritual maturity than you, experience in mentoring or discipling others, and time to meet with you regularly (one or two times a month). He or she should also be someone you can trust with private matters, probably someone of the same gender (because of the level of closeness that will develop). For more information, see chapters 7–9 of *Working the Angles* by Eugene Peterson mentioned in the Suggested Reading list.

STUDY 7: THE SABBATH

Purpose:
- To see in a fresh way that the Lord's Day is a joy, the best day of the week.
- To brainstorm new, practical ideas for observing the Sabbath this week.

Question 3. The Sabbath institution involved rest for slaves and servants as well as masters, freeing everyone from constant work (see Deuteronomy 5:12-15). "Maintain justice and do what is right" can be seen as a summary of the Law (see Exodus 19:5, Deuteronomy 6:4-5, and Micah 6:8). The Sabbath is a specific, symbolic example, as seen in Ezekiel 22:8 and 23:38

(adapted from John D. W. Watts, *Isaiah: Word Biblical Commentary,* vol. 25, Waco: Word, 1987).

Question 4. Eunuchs (men who were castrated) and foreigners were excluded from the worship services of God's people (see Deuteronomy 23:1,3,7-8); in other words, they were outcasts.

Question 5. Take some time to discuss the burden of a 24/7, always-on-call, always-plugged-in lifestyle. Ideas include turning off the cell phone, computer, and television for twenty-four hours, not because they are wrong, but because they interfere with Sabbath.

Question 7. Far from being "exclude[d] from [God's] people" and a "dry tree" (verse 3), these outcasts were invited to take part in the Sabbath—the central element of life among God's people. Today, single persons, divorced persons, disabled persons, street people, internationals, and others may find it difficult to be fully involved in a church because members are afraid or are uncertain how to welcome them (see James 2:1-4). Help the group probe the implications of this passage for ministering to marginalized people today. What can you do to bring them into the central worship and ministry of the local church?

Question 9. Note the parallel phrases "as you please" and "your own way" in Isaiah 58:13. Consider how seeking selfish pleasure would get in the way of the delights and joys of the Sabbath. The contrast here is not our own pleasure versus Sabbath pain, but rather our pleasure versus the joy that God wants to give us.

Question 11. As the group brainstorms ways to delight in the Sabbath, suggest the following: Set aside fifteen minutes before leaving for church to meditate on a praise psalm; develop a small singing group to enrich worship services; go for a walk in the woods after browsing through a book of landscape paintings; spend the afternoon with your Bible study group, singing, walking, or preparing a meal together.

It may be helpful to discuss alternate days for Sabbath rest. "Sabbath" does not always mean "Sunday." While most Christian churches worship on Sunday, many people have no control over their work shifts on Sunday. Suggest the possibility of having mini-Sabbaths during a pressure-filled week.

Study 8: Worship

Purpose:
- To understand that worship brings us into God's presence.
- To experience this presence in a new way with other believers as we gather to worship on the coming Lord's Day.

Question 2. Hebrews 12:18-21 describes the scene on Mount Sinai when God gave the Ten Commandments to Moses (see Exodus 19:16-19).

Question 5. Hebrews 12:22-24 refers to Mount Zion, a name for Jerusalem and a symbol of the presence of God, or of heaven. Focus attention on the words *terrifying* (verse 21) and *joyful* (verse 22) as you contrast the two scenes.

Question 8. Christ's death on the cross ("sprinkled blood") for our sins makes all the difference in our relationship with God. He is our Savior and Mediator, enabling us to approach God in joyful worship rather than in fear of judgment. (See also Hebrews 4:14–10:39, where the effect of Christ's death is explained in detail.)

Question 10. There is a sense in which we, in Christ, are already seated "in the heavenly realms" (Ephesians 2:6), especially when we gather for corporate worship in the church. Apply this truth to your weekly church service, which may seem ho-hum and routine, without any real awareness of God's presence or the gathered unseen host mentioned in our passage. Twenty-first-century Christians are conditioned by scientism and naturalism ("what you see is what you get"), especially when we try to understand the unseen presence of God. Believers must transcend the limitations imposed by these popular worldviews in order to worship God effectively.

Suggested Reading

Coleman, Robert E. *The Master Plan of Discipleship*. Grand Rapids: Revell, 1998.

Dawn, Marva J. *Keeping the Sabbath Wholly: Ceasing, Resting, Embracing, Feasting*. Grand Rapids: Eerdmans, 1989.

Foster, Richard J. *Celebration of Discipline*. San Francisco: HarperSanFrancisco, 2002.

Lathrop, Gordon W. *Holy Things: A Liturgical Theology*. Minneapolis: Fortress, 1998.

McPherson, C. W. *Keeping Silence: Christian Practices for Entering Stillness*. Harrisburg, Pa.: Morehouse, 2002.

Nouwen, Henri J. M. *The Way of the Heart: Desert Spirituality and Contemporary Ministry*. San Francisco: HarperSanFrancisco, 1991.

Old, Hughes Oliphant. *Leading in Prayer: A Workbook for Worship*. Grand Rapids: Eerdmans, 1995.

Peterson, Eugene. *Working the Angles: The Shape of Pastoral Integrity*. Grand Rapids: Eerdmans, 1987.

Toon, Peter. *Meditating As a Christian*. San Francisco: HarperSanFrancisco, 1991.

What Should We Study Next?

I f you enjoyed this Fisherman Bible Studyguide, you might want to explore our full line of Fisherman Resources and Bible Studyguides. The following books offer time-tested Fisherman inductive Bible studies for individuals or groups.

FISHERMAN RESOURCES

The Art of Spiritual Listening: Responding to God's Voice Amid the Noise of Life by Alice Fryling
Balm in Gilead by Dudley Delffs
The Essential Bible Guide by Whitney T. Kuniholm
Questions from the God Who Needs No Answers: What Is He Really Asking of You? by Carolyn and Craig Williford
Reckless Faith: Living Passionately as Imperfect Christians by Jo Kadlecek
Soul Strength: Spiritual Courage for the Battles of Life by Pam Lau

FISHERMAN BIBLE STUDYGUIDES

Topical Studies
Angels by Vinita Hampton Wright
Becoming Women of Purpose by Ruth Haley Barton
Building Your House on the Lord: A Firm Foundation for Family Life (Revised Edition) by Steve and Dee Brestin

Discipleship: The Growing Christian's Lifestyle by James and
   Martha Reapsome
*Doing Justice, Showing Mercy: Christian Action in Today's
   World* by Vinita Hampton Wright
Encouraging Others: Biblical Models for Caring by Lin Johnson
The End Times: Discovering What the Bible Says by E. Michael
   Rusten
Examining the Claims of Jesus by Dee Brestin
Friendship: Portraits in God's Family Album by Steve and
   Dee Brestin
The Fruit of the Spirit: Growing in Christian Character by
   Stuart Briscoe
Great Doctrines of the Bible by Stephen Board
Great Passages of the Bible by Carol Plueddemann
Great Prayers of the Bible by Carol Plueddemann
Growing Through Life's Challenges by James and Martha
   Reapsome
Guidance & God's Will by Tom and Joan Stark
Heart Renewal: Finding Spiritual Refreshment by Ruth Goring
Higher Ground: Steps Toward Christian Maturity by Steve and
   Dee Brestin
Images of Redemption: God's Unfolding Plan Through the Bible
   by Ruth E. Van Reken
Integrity: Character from the Inside Out by Ted W. Engstrom
   and Robert C. Larson
Lifestyle Priorities by John White
Marriage: Learning from Couples in Scripture by R. Paul and
   Gail Stevens
Miracles by Robbie Castleman
One Body, One Spirit: Building Relationships in the Church by
   Dale and Sandy Larsen

The Parables of Jesus by Gladys Hunt
Parenting with Purpose and Grace by Alice Fryling
Prayer: Discovering What Scripture Says by Timothy Jones and
Jill Zook-Jones
The Prophets: God's Truth Tellers by Vinita Hampton Wright
Proverbs and Parables: God's Wisdom for Living by Dee
Brestin
Satisfying Work: Christian Living from Nine to Five by R. Paul
Stevens and Gerry Schoberg
Senior Saints: Growing Older in God's Family by James and
Martha Reapsome
The Sermon on the Mount: The God Who Understands Me by
Gladys M. Hunt
Speaking Wisely: Exploring the Power of Words by Poppy
Smith
Spiritual Disciplines: The Tasks of a Joyful Life by Larry Sibley
Spiritual Gifts by Karen Dockrey
Spiritual Hunger: Filling Your Deepest Longings by Jim and
Carol Plueddemann
A Spiritual Legacy: Faith for the Next Generation by Chuck
and Winnie Christensen
Spiritual Warfare by A. Scott Moreau
The Ten Commandments: God's Rules for Living by Stuart
Briscoe
Ultimate Hope for Changing Times by Dale and Sandy Larsen
When Faith Is All You Have: A Study of Hebrews 11 by Ruth
E. Van Reken
Where Your Treasure Is: What the Bible Says About Money by
James and Martha Reapsome
Who Is God? by David P. Seemuth
Who Is Jesus? In His Own Words by Ruth E. Van Reken

Who Is the Holy Spirit? by Barbara H. Knuckles and Ruth
    E. Van Reken

Wisdom for Today's Woman: Insights from Esther by Poppy
    Smith

Witnesses to All the World: God's Heart for the Nations by Jim
    and Carol Plueddemann

Women at Midlife: Embracing the Challenges by Jeanie Miley

Worship: Discovering What Scripture Says by Larry Sibley

Bible Book Studies

Genesis: Walking with God by Margaret Fromer and Sharrel
    Keyes

Exodus: God Our Deliverer by Dale and Sandy Larsen

Ruth: Relationships That Bring Life by Ruth Haley Barton

Ezra and Nehemiah: A Time to Rebuild by James Reapsome

(For Esther, see Topical Studies, *Wisdom for Today's Woman*)

Job: Trusting Through Trials by Ron Klug

Psalms: A Guide to Prayer and Praise by Ron Klug

Proverbs: Wisdom That Works by Vinita Hampton Wright

Ecclesiastes: A Time for Everything by Stephen Board

Song of Songs: A Dialogue of Intimacy by James Reapsome

Jeremiah: The Man and His Message by James Reapsome

Jonah, Habakkuk, and Malachi: Living Responsibly by
    Margaret Fromer and Sharrel Keyes

Matthew: People of the Kingdom by Larry Sibley

Mark: God in Action by Chuck and Winnie Christensen

Luke: Following Jesus by Sharrel Keyes

John: The Living Word by Whitney Kuniholm

Acts 1–12: God Moves in the Early Church by Chuck and
    Winnie Christensen

Acts 13–28, see *Paul* under Character Studies
Romans: The Christian Story by James Reapsome
1 Corinthians: Problems and Solutions in a Growing Church by
Charles and Ann Hummel
Strengthened to Serve: 2 Corinthians by Jim and Carol
Plueddemann
Galatians, Titus, and Philemon: Freedom in Christ by Whitney
Kuniholm
Ephesians: Living in God's Household by Robert Baylis
Philippians: God's Guide to Joy by Ron Klug
Colossians: Focus on Christ by Luci Shaw
Letters to the Thessalonians by Margaret Fromer and Sharrel
Keyes
Letters to Timothy: Discipleship in Action by Margaret Fromer
and Sharrel Keyes
Hebrews: Foundations for Faith by Gladys Hunt
James: Faith in Action by Chuck and Winnie Christensen
1 and 2 Peter, Jude: Called for a Purpose by Steve and Dee
Brestin
1, 2, 3 John: How Should a Christian Live? by Dee Brestin
Revelation: The Lamb Who Is the Lion by Gladys Hunt

Bible Character Studies
Abraham: Model of Faith by James Reapsome
David: Man After God's Own Heart by Robbie Castleman
Elijah: Obedience in a Threatening World by Robbie
Castleman
Great People of the Bible by Carol Plueddemann
King David: Trusting God for a Lifetime by Robbie
Castleman

Men Like Us: Ordinary Men, Extraordinary God by Paul
    Heidebrecht and Ted Scheuermann
Moses: Encountering God by Greg Asimakoupoulos
Paul: Thirteenth Apostle (Acts 13–28) by Chuck and Winnie
    Christensen
Women Like Us: Wisdom for Today's Issues by Ruth Haley
    Barton
Women Who Achieved for God by Winnie Christensen
Women Who Believed God by Winnie Christensen